HOW TO BECOME A

RAINMAKER

HOW TO BECOME A
RAINMAKER

*The People
Who Get
and
Keep Customers*

JEFFREY J. FOX

Vermilion
LONDON

First published in the United States in 2000 by Hyperion
Published by arrangement with Doris S. Michaels Literary Agency
First published in the United Kingdom in 2001 by Vermilion
an imprint of Ebury Press
Random House, 20 Vauxhall Bridge Road, London SW1V 2SA

Random House Australia (Pty) Limited
20 Alfred Street, Milsons Point, Sydney,
New South Wales 2061, Australia

Random House New Zealand Limited
18 Poland Road, Glenfield,
Auckland 10, New Zealand

Random House (Pty) Limited
Endulini, 5A Jubilee Road, Parktown 2193, South Africa

The Random House Group Limited Reg. No. 954009
www.randomhouse.co.uk

A CIP catalogue record for this book is available from the British Library

ISBN 0 09187654 0

Printed and bound in Great Britain by Mackays of Chatham

Papers used by Vermilion are natural, recyclable products
made from wood grown in sustainable forests

Dedicated to
Catherine M. Fox
and to
Dorothy and Modesto Brunoli
"Because Rainmakers sometimes need
umbrellas"

ACKNOWLEDGMENTS

Thanks to:

My sharp-penciled and sharp-witted editor,
Mary Ellen O'Neill, and to all the enthusiastic
people at Hyperion.

My indefatigable agents at the Doris S. Michaels
Literary Agency, Inc., in New York City.

The hardworking folks at Fox & Co. who teach
rainmaking every day.

And, especially, to the source for Chapter 32.

CONTENTS

CONTENTS

CONTENTS

CONTENTS

CONTENTS

CONTENTS

CONTENTS

CONTENTS

CONTENTS

HOW TO BECOME A
RAINMAKER

INTRODUCTION

You Should Read This Book If Your Organization Needs Revenues

*A*merican Indian tradition exalts the Rain-maker. The Rainmaker used magical powers to bring the rain to nourish the crops to feed the people. Without the rain, the people would weaken, die, or have to move elsewhere.

Today, a Rainmaker is a person who brings revenue into an organization, be it profit or not-for-profit. That revenue comes from customers and donors. That revenue is the *aqua viva*—the lifeblood—of the organization. Without it the organization will die.

Customers' money is the rain.

The term *Rainmaker* is more commonly used in such professional service industries as legal, accounting, consulting, investment banking, advertising, and architecture. In these industries, Rainmakers are the two or so people in the firm who are responsible for generating most of the new customers, the new business.

Big-hitting Rainmakers are among the highest paid employees in every company in every industry. They operate under many titles: owner, partner, chancellor, sales representative, CEO, agent, managing director, and fund-raiser. If becoming a Rainmaker is your goal, then this book will help you get there.

There is another kind of Rainmaker, and he or she is an employee—or associate or colleague or team member or crew member. Every employee must be somehow involved in the identification, attraction, getting, and keeping of customers. The advice in this book tilts to the salesperson, but if you have contact with customers, or work with and support colleagues who have contact with customers, this book will make you more effective. You will be better able to sell inside, to sell your ideas to your organization.

The most important success factor in any business or organization is having a customer. This is more important than the business idea, the products, the machinery, the buildings, the financing, or the people. It is customer money that pays everyone's salary, that pays for pension plans, union dues, bonuses, vacations, health insurance, computers, and office furniture. Customers are known by many names: members, students, fans, soldiers, parishioners, and patients. Regardless of what they are called, without customers no organization can continue to survive.

Therefore, the paramount job of every single employee in an organization is to, directly or indirectly, get and keep customers. This is true without exception!

The job of every employee is to help ring the cash register. The job of every employee is to keep the customers coming, and to keep the customers coming back.

This book is a recipe for how to sell, for how to make rain, be it drizzle or deluge, sprinkle or storm. If your organization needs revenues, and if you want to become invaluable to your organization, then read this book.

• I •

The Rainmaker's Credo

- Cherish customers at all times.
- Treat customers as you would your best friend.
- Listen to customers and decipher their needs.
- Make (or give) customers what they need.
- Price your product to its dollarized* value.

*Although in the UK we use pounds sterling we'll stick with the author's concept of 'dollarize'.

- Show customers the dollarized value of what they will get.
- Teach customers to want what they need.
- Make your product the way customers want it.
- Get your product to your customers when they want it.
- Give your customers a little extra, more than they expect.
- Remind customers of the dollarized value they received.
- Thank each customer sincerely and often.
- Help customers pay you, so they won't be embarrassed and go elsewhere.
- Ask to do it again.

• II •

Always Answer the Question, "Why Should This Customer Do Business with Us?"

Never make a sales call on a customer unless you can answer the question "Why should this customer do business with our company, with me?" The answer must be a benefit to the customer. The answer must fit the customer's agenda, not yours. The customer should do business with you because you will make him feel good, or you will solve his problem, or both. There must be a business benefit and a personal benefit—often interlinked—for the customer.

For example, a business benefit might be getting a new product to market sooner, thereby generating millions of pounds in new sales. The personal benefit might be a job promotion for the customer.

If the benefit makes the customer feel good, then, for example, the effective furnace or natural gas salesperson's answer might be "The customer will get warm, cozy rooms." (The ineffective furnace salesperson thinks the customer is buying BTUs.) If your product solves a problem then the answer to the question should be phrased in pounds and pence. For example, assume a software program enables a hotel to more accurately cap-ture and bill any computer usage of hotel phone lines. If that's the case, the reason the customer should do business with you is because your prod-uct will generate £2 per room per night in incre-mental revenue.

The Rainmaker answers the question "Why should the customer do business with us?" by calculating what economic benefits the product will give the customer and by calculating the consequences to the customer of not going with the recommended product. The Rainmaker determines how the customer is benefited directly and personally.

The Rainmaker puts himself or herself in the customer's shoes and answers the question "If I were the customer, how would this product benefit me?"

• III •

Obey Marketing's First Commandment

*T*he first commandment of getting and keeping customers is to treat each customer as you would treat yourself. Do you like to be overcharged, underserved, put on endless hold, overbooked, told your room isn't ready, falsely promised, shipped late, ignored, not thanked?

Always put yourself in the shoes of the good customer. Answer the question "What would I want if I were the customer?" The answer is what you should strive to provide.

This is important when dealing with the upset customer. When you are the upset customer, you want a full, uninterrupted hearing, you want to deal with someone with the authority to fix the problem, and you want a fair resolution. You don't want to be sent a copy of the company's warranty policy. You don't want to be told to send another sample of your upholstery to the factory, get yet another professional couch cleaning, or be told the stains are of "indeterminate nature" and your claim is denied.

Remember, good customers are demanding. They may expect more from you than you believe is appropriate. What you want or how you want to be treated may not be good enough to satisfy your customers, but it's a good starting place.

Deliver on your promise and you'll bring rain.

• IV •

Customers Don't Care About You

*I*n the selling arena, customers don't care if you have a mortgage to pay. Customers don't care if you need their business to win a contest. Customers don't care why your shipments are late. Customers don't care what you like, where you went to school, or what sports you play or played.

The only thing customers care about are themselves and their problem. You are in front of the customer only because the customer believes, if only a little bit, that you might be able to better his or her situation.

You are there by invitation only. You must concentrate on the customer. You must be on high receive. You do not talk about yourself; rather, you ask probing, preplanned questions. You listen to what the customer says. Clarify. Summarize. Determine how you can help the customer and how your product solves the customer's concern.

Rainmakers say "you"; they don't say "I."

• V •

Always Precall Plan Every Sales Call

*A*ppointments with decision makers are relatively rare events. Meetings with decision makers are crucial to getting the sale. Because of this, meetings with a decision maker must be carefully preplanned. Precall planning is particularly important when making the first call on a new customer *and* when making the last call—the one that concludes with an order.

Ninety percent of all sales calls are won or lost before the salesperson sees the customer. This is because so few salespeople actually plan the call. Too many salespeople believe experience is a substitute for precall planning; they think they don't need to. Other salespeople do their precall planning on the way to a call. Others don't even know how to precall plan. Some don't know they should.

Rainmakers never waste a sales call: They always precall plan. It is typical for a Rainmaker to spend three hours planning for a fifteen-minute sales call. Planning and practicing for two days to two weeks for a single sales call is not uncommon.

One Rainmaker spent fifteen straight eight-hour days researching and planning a fifteen-minute sales call. The call was on the CEO of a leading company in a new industry. If this company adopted the Rainmaker's product, almost certainly the other companies in the industry would follow. The Rainmaker made the sale and successfully used it as a case history to close other customers. This single sale saved the Rainmaker's company and led to years of success.

NFL coaches spend countless hours reviewing game films in preparation for their next opponent. It is said that if Joe Paterno, the heralded head coach of the Penn State football team, is given two weeks to develop a game plan, his team is nearly invincible.

A precall plan for a Rainmaker is like a preflight check for an airplane pilot. The great pilots never miss a single checkpoint before taking off or landing. If a pilot misses something, that pilot may be missing. If a salesperson misses something, the order may be missing.

A precall planning checklist should include:

1. Written sales call objective.

2. Needs analysis questions to ask.

3. Something to show.

4. Anticipated customer concerns and objections.

5. Points of difference vis-à-vis competitors.

6. Meaningful benefits to customers.

7. Dollarization approach; investment return analysis.

8. Strategies to handle objections and eliminate customer concerns.

9. Closing strategies.

10. Expected surprises.

And plan to be flexible. If after sixty seconds into your two-hour painstakingly prepared presentation the customer says she will buy, stop talking, take the order, and gracefully leave. If the customer wants to do business with you, but in an entirely different manner than you expected, adjust to the change. Don't be so intent on following your plan that you miss a customer's cue. Be flexible.

A Rainmaker never calls on a decision maker without a written precall plan.

• VI •

Fish Where the Big Fish Are

*W*hen asked "What is the most important thing you need when you go fishing?" most people say "bait," "pole," "hooks," and "beer." Those are important, but the most important thing needed is fish! You can have the best boat on the prettiest lake with awesome tackle, but if there are no fish, you will go home empty-handed. If, however, you have only a raggedy old net but a little pond teeming with fish, your chances of a catch are much greater.

Where you cast your line is crucial to catching fish. This is also true for selling. Rainmakers fish where the big fish are. Rainmakers talk to customers who are familiar with their product, or who already use the product, or who have a high probability of using the product. Don't waste your time trying to convince dairy farmers to buy horseshoes. And don't waste your time selling hospital beds to hotels.

Big companies in an industry are generally better prospects than small companies in the same industry. Successful customers are generally better prospects than struggling customers. Customers who want your product are better targets than customers who need your product. (Customers who need your product may not know it. They must be educated, persuaded. This takes time and money. Customers who want your product are partially sold before they see you.)

To a Rainmaker, the big sale is the trophy fish on the wall.

• VII •

Show Them the Money!

*C*ustomers buy for only two reasons: to feel good or to solve a problem. Going out to dinner, buying scuba equipment, or getting a new puppy fall into the "feel good" category. The prevailing purchase motivation for organizations is to solve a problem. The solution to the problem can *always* be expressed in financial terms—in pounds and pence. If a company invests £100,000 in advertising, they expect that advertising to generate £500,000 in sales. When a motor manufacturer replaces a cheap £.08 rubber o-ring with a £.10 viton o-ring, they expect to save £.30 per o-ring with reduced warranty claims. A tree surgeon uses a £900 saw because it cuts five times faster than a cheaper saw, saving him £50 a day in reduced labor costs.

Rainmakers don't sell fasteners or valves or washing machines or double-paned windows or tax audits or irrigation systems or training programs or golf clubs. *Rainmakers sell money!* They sell reduced downtime, fewer repairs, better gas mileage, higher deposit interest, increased output, decreased energy usage, more wheat per acre, more yardage per swing.

Rainmakers help the customer see the money. Rainmakers turn benefits into dollars. The plumber who generates the most revenue doesn't charge £50 for a service call, he sells a clean, dry basement for £100, saving the customer's thousand-dollar carpet.

The lock salesperson doesn't sell locks, he sells security for valuables. The pool salesman doesn't just sell recreation, he sells an increase in home value.

The number one salesperson for a company that made cough medicine never sold a single bottle of cough medicine. He was by far the leading salesperson, but he never sold a cough drop.

The company made products for people with colds, sore throats, hay fever, and sinus conditions. The company made throat lozenges, cough drops, gargles, and sprays. The company trained its sales force on how the products worked, all about the product chemistry, and why their products were the best. The company's success depended on how many cases of cough medicine and gargle it sold. That meant the company's success depended on the demand for the product; the number of people with colds.

The company made its product available to the public by selling to pharmacies, to drugstore owners. In order to make its products more appealing to the drugstore owner than the competitors' medicine, the salesperson's company offered an incentive: For every five cases of products purchased the druggist could either get one case of product for free (to resell at retail prices) or a cash check for the equivalent purchase price of one case. (The free case or check were both worth £25.)

The salesperson realized that his customers were not people with colds. His customers were the drugstore owners. (People with colds were the druggists' customers.) So despite all the technical product training, unlike his colleagues, the number one salesperson never talked about the products' formulas, strength, or soothing aspects.

The number one salesperson talked to the drugstore owners about money.

The salesperson explained the five-case purchase incentive, asking the drugstore owners if they would prefer the free product or the money (in a bank check). Almost always, the drugstore owners would opt for the money.

The salesperson didn't sell cures for coughs, he sold a rebate check of £25 for every five cases of product purchased. After the drugstore owner agreed to take the money, the salesperson would ask, "How much money would you like?" Getting more money meant buying more product, and that's what many pharmacists did.

The number one salesperson sold money! All the other salespeople regaled druggists with facts on cough suppressant chemicals and breathe-free passages. They were far-distant followers in the contest.

Always show the customer the money. Always dollarize (see "A Rainmaker Extra," page 148). Quantify the customer's return on his investment in your product. Calculate the financial consequences to the customer—the cost of going without your solution.

Rainmakers don't sell products; they sell the dollarized value the customer gets from the products.

Rainmakers sell money.

• VIII •

Earthquakes Don't Count

You either made the sale or you didn't.

No one wants to hear why you didn't bring in the business. No one cares that "the peso was devalued," or "the customer went bankrupt," or "the economy is lousy," or "a huge competitor opened next door."

The hunter either comes home with the game or he doesn't. His family eats or goes hungry. No one cares that "the rain washed away the deer tracks."

A young brand manager captured the attention of his company's sales force by offering terrific prizes for hitting defined sales quotas. The contest rules were easy: reach your quota, you win; fall short, you lose. Three weeks before the contest deadline an earthquake hit Los Angeles. The California sales office was badly damaged and business was interrupted. The California sales team did not reach its quota.

California was the largest market in the brand manager's company. The California sales team had great influence in the company. The California sales team wanted the prizes, but the brand manager said no. The California sales team used all its muscle, and the powerful vice president of sales insisted the brand manager award California the prizes. The vice president argued that the California team missed its quota by "only a few percentage points" and "be reasonable. . .there was an earthquake."

The brand manager firmly stood his ground, and replied, "Earthquakes don't count."

The next year there were record blizzards in Chicago, floods along the Mississippi, a brownout in New York City, a natural gas shortage and political crises in Washington. The next year every region in the country hit its quota—California came in first—and everyone won a prize.

Rainmakers don't have excuses.

• IX •

Killer Sales Question #1

*O*ne of the four events that are inherent in every sale is scheduling an appointment with the decision maker. You can't get the sale unless you talk to the decision maker. Getting appointments with busy decision makers is often difficult. Phone sellers often make preliminary calls to set up a phone conference, the appointment. Field salespeople know there is no substitute for the face-to-face meeting.

Do the homework. Dollarize the reason why

the customer should do business with you. Send a four- or five-sentence letter to the customer detailing the dollarized benefit of the product and promising a follow-up phone call. The objective of the letter is to get the customer to take the follow-up phone call. Good customers don't ignore a compelling dollarization. They will take your call.

When you have the customer on the phone, suggest a meeting, and then ask, "Do you have your appointment calendar handy?"

This is a killer sales question because it leads to that precious appointment over 90 percent of the time.

Then ask, "Is Tuesday at three OK?" "No." "How about Thursday at eight-thirty A.M.?" "No." "How about next Friday at three?" "Fine." "OK, great, the meeting will take about twenty minutes. See you at three. Thanks."

Rainmakers make appointments to make rain.

Always Take the Best Seat
in a Restaurant

*I*f you take a customer or prospective customer to breakfast, lunch, or dinner, always take the best seat. You take the seat with your back to the wall. You take the seat that looks out onto the golf course or marina or street. You don't want your customer's attention to wander. You don't want your customer to check out who is coming and going.

You want your customer to focus on you. You want your customer as involved as possible in answering your questions and evaluating your recommendations. You do not want his concentration or his considerations interrupted by someone or something more interesting than your software package or office machine or mutual fund or design proposal or refrigeration equipment.

Your customer has invested some of his precious time to meet with you. It is only polite for you to optimize his time investment, and not let it be squandered by distractions.

If the customer takes you to breakfast, lunch, or dinner, you still take the best seat.

• XI •

Don't Drink Coffee
on a Sales Call

A sales call is a sales call. It's not teatime at the Rainbow Room. You are not there to "wake up and smell the coffee." You are there to do business.

The duration of the average sales call is eighteen to twenty minutes. You do not have time to go get the coffee, pour the coffee, stir in the cream, or drink the coffee. You have to maximize time and concentrate on your objective. Drinking coffee wastes time and interferes with your presentation. You can't take notes with a coffee cup in your hand.

A sales call was scheduled three months in advance. It was difficult to get an appointment with the harried decision maker who was responsible for buying high-ticket (over £180,000 a copy) computer peripheral packages. The salesperson and a consultant to his company met for breakfast to preplan the sales call. When offered, the salesperson said he did not drink coffee.

The duo arrived promptly and was met by the prospective customer, the Computer Center Manager. The customer was friendly and graciously asked if his guests would like some coffee. "That would be great," said the salesperson who did not drink coffee. So off they trudged to the coffee room, and began the ritual. They returned to the customer's office. The salesperson put his coffee on the worktable, but accidentally set the cup on a blueprint-marking pen. The coffee spilled over the worktable. The customer scrambled to save the blueprints. Paper towels were needed.

The sales call ultimately restarted. Ten minutes into the call everything looked promising: The customer was in agreement, he had a need for the package, and he had the budget. There was a knock on the door and someone from the Computer Center anxiously told the manager that "one of the main servers is in a degraded mode!" The prospective customer jumped to his feet and, while politely excusing himself, invited the salesperson to phone in a few weeks to see if they could reschedule. And out the door vanished the customer. . .and the sale.

Coffee killed that sale.

If the customer asks if you want coffee, say "no, thank you" and get to work.

And don't drink coffee on the plane, or in the car, on the way to a sales call. A spill can kill.

• XII •

You're Not at Lunch
to Eat Lunch

*I*f you are at a cocktail party with customers, you are not there to party. If you are playing golf with a client, you are not there to play golf.

These are business meetings or sales calls or both. You do business at business meetings. Some salespeople forget the priority. They actually care what golf score they shoot. And at the nineteenth hole, instead of closing the deal, they are still talking about the thirty-five-foot putt they made on the front nine.

A luncheon meeting with a client or prospective customer is a sales call with tableware. You are there to ask questions, to listen, and to get a commitment. You are not there to sample the bronzed shrimp Creole or do research for a restaurant review. Don't waste time perusing the intricacies of the menu. Don't ask the waiter how anything is prepared. Don't ask the waitress if a rasher of bacon is three strips or four. Food is not your focus—the customer is!

Order something easy to eat. Order only one course. Order something inexpensive.

It is OK if you don't eat anything. It is rude to talk with food in your mouth. It is impolite to survey your dish when your customer is talking. And it is hard to take notes with a fork in your hand.

It's not about lunch. It's about getting the customer's commitment, getting the bill, and getting on to the next appointment.

• XIII •

Never Wear a Pen in Your Shirt Pocket

*I*t's your first meeting with a prospective client. You prepared carefully. You dressed with care. You are ready to persuade the customer to do business with you because of your meticulous attention to detail.

Your designer pen, in your left breast pocket, has bled. A startling blue stain has become a focal point for your customer. She can't take her eyes off your ruined shirt. She can't get completely involved in your presentation. She feels trapped.

She is embarrassed for you. She is too polite to tell you, and is nervous about what to do when you discover the leak. She is hoping the meeting will end quickly. She is hoping to avoid witnessing your inevitable discomfort.

Your leaky pen killed the sale.

And you don't want ballpoint streaks on your shirt, either. Buy shirts without pockets, and keep your pens in your briefcase.

Rainmakers do nothing that might decrease the odds of making the sale.

• XIV •

Killer Sales Question #2

*A*fter exhaustive homework and a careful needs analysis, the Rainmaker knows if he has a solution to the customer's problem. The Rainmaker has dollarized the solution and knows how much money the customer will get from the solution, and how much it will cost the customer to go without the solution.

The Rainmaker understands that sometimes a customer will ignore the facts, or will stay disengaged from the decision-making process, resulting in a "no sale." The customer must be engaged, and must be in agreement.

To get the customer involved, and to begin the necessary chain of positive agreements and commitments, the Rainmaker asks a powerful question that taps into the sense of free will and independence that is part of human nature.

The Rainmaker asks the customer, "Based on analysis, it looks like you can save £110,000 per year with the solution. Can I assume there are probably a number of things that have to be done before you are completely comfortable with this approach? OK, so before we get into this in any depth, can I get your agreement on the analysis? Will you look at the facts and decide for yourself if they make sense?"

This is a killer sales question.

To say to the customer "will you decide for yourself?" is almost rhetorical because the answer is so seemingly obvious. The customer is certainly going to decide for herself. So she will answer yes, and will silently think, perhaps say aloud, "Of course I will decide for myself."

If the facts bear out the salesperson's claim of saving £110,000, then for the customer to reject the solution, she must contradict her answer and admit she can't decide for herself. This is an admission most customers won't make.

By agreeing to decide for herself, the customer eliminates the option of not deciding. The customer is now engaged and can't ignore the facts. One way or another, the customer will make a decision. If the solution benefits her—as it must— she will buy.

Rainmakers Turn Customer Objections into Customer Objectives

*C*ustomers always have concerns or issues that must be satisfied before they will buy. Customers are concerned about price, affordability, delivery, reliability, size, color, warranty, availability, and myriad other issues. These concerns are sometimes spoken and sometimes not. These concerns vary by customer and vary in importance. A concern that is a deal breaker to one customer is a detail to another. These concerns are prepurchase objections to the salesperson's proposal, whatever it may be. When the customer says, "The motor is too loud," he is objecting to the noise of the product. When the customer says, "I don't like forest green," she is objecting to the color.

Rainmakers welcome customer objections because they know objections are simply the way customers express their desires. The Rainmaker knows that when the customer says, "Your price is too high," the customer's goal is to get the proper value for the money invested. The objection tells the Rainmaker that the customer does not yet have enough information to make a positive buying decision.

The Rainmaker always turns a customer objection into a mutual—customer/Rainmaker—objective. The Rainmaker, in question form, restates the customer's objection as an objective. To illustrate: The customer says, "Your delivery time is too long." The Rainmaker responds, "So our objective is to get you the product when you want it, correct?"

Only Rainmakers understand the brilliant subtlety of turning objections into objectives. First, this technique changes the tone of the language from adversarial to positive. Second, the customer's yes response is an agreement—an invitation to continue the discussion. Third, the Rainmaker can now ask more questions to perfectly understand the customer's concern and to move to a mutually acceptable solution. For example, the Rainmaker might ask, "When exactly do you need the product?" Then say, "If you will commit today to a six-month purchase agreement, we can forecast monthly shipments, thereby ensuring that you will get the product on the first of the month, every month. Why don't we give this a try for six months?"

Rainmakers believe that objections are the way customers mask pleas for help and information. Rainmakers encourage objections, especially the hidden or unspoken ones. Rainmakers know that the sale cannot be made until every customer concern, no matter how trivial it seems, is satisfactorily handled. Consequently, if the sale is not made, Rainmakers always ask, "Is there anything else that concerns you?" Or, "What else may be prohibiting us from moving ahead?"

Rainmakers always probe for objections. Rainmakers love objections.

• XVI •

Always Make a "Mid-Job, Next-Job" Recommendation

*T*he Rainmaker is always thinking about how his company can help the customer, how the customer's sales, profits, or well-being can be bettered. The Rainmaker knows that the customer's continuing success is the only basis for the Rainmaker's success.

The Rainmaker is always alert for the next job, the next assignment, the next sale. The Rainmaker knows that the easiest next sale is to a

current customer. Current customers know the
seller; they have an emotional investment in him
and in his company. After all, the customer took
a risk and hired or bought product from the Rainmaker's company. The customer knows if the
Rainmaker and his firm delivered on their promise. If the Rainmaker's company successfully delivered the solution, the customer is grateful.
Grateful customers are loyal customers.

Midway through one project with a customer,
the Rainmaker proposes another way in which the
Rainmaker's company can help the customer.
This is the "mid-job, next-job" memo or recommendation letter. Presenting a "mid-job, next-
job" memo is a Rainmaker rule.

The landscaper, in the midst of sodding the
yard, suggests a rock wall to reduce runoff and to
enhance the property. The caterer, overwhelm-
ingly busy serving a summer party, reminds her
host that Christmas is only five months away. The
lawyer, submerged in the details of a complicated

estate plan, asks her client if her firm can do the client's upcoming house purchase closing.

Your customer doesn't know all you can do for her. Only you know. By the time you are halfway through your current job you should know how else you can help your customer. When you are in the middle of a job, begin selling the next one.

Rainmakers always have a mid-job, next-job action plan.

• XVII •

Treat Everybody You Meet as a Potential Client

Rainmakers see the world, and everyone in it, as their market. Rainmakers know the world is small. They know that everyone knows someone. They know that anyone can become a client, or refer a client, or recommend a client, or scuttle a promising relationship.

Rainmakers treat nonclients as they do existing customers. They are polite to everyone. Rainmakers view everyone as influential. They know that business can come from unexpected places.

They know that something they did ten years ago might result in business today.

There are no "little people" to the Rainmaker. They do not berate the waiter because the kitchen is slow. They do not get angry with the person at the ticket counter because the airline delays or cancels a flight. Everyone is treated with courtesy. The Rainmaker is as respectful and polite to the guy who mows his lawn as he is to the president of the company that makes the lawn mowers.

A wire and cable salesman had a good relationship with the top management of a client company in Florida. The first person he met on every sales call at this customer was the company's receptionist, an efficient, organized young woman. Part of her job was keeping the sales appointment schedule. Although she was not the person who bought wire and cable, and was never involved in the decision making, the salesman always treated her courteously. The salesman always waited patiently if there were delays, never making insistent demands—as did other salespeople. The salesman never implied his importance by dropping the name of the executive vice president, the person he was there to see, as did others. The salesman always thanked the receptionist for her help, and always made sure to say good-bye to her.

Eighteen years later, the receptionist is now the executive vice president of the company. With her influence, her company became the wire and cable salesman's biggest account.

Don't make unnecessary enemies. Why be unlikable? Who is ever helped by unpleasant behavior? Pleasant people often appear self-controlled and confident. Customers like that.

The Rainmaker knows that anybody can help or hurt.

• XVIII •

Heed the Biggest Buy Signal

A "buy signal" is something a customer does that indicates his or her willingness to purchase. When you ask a group of salespeople to state the biggest (most important) buy signals, they will usually list "the customer smiles," "the customer asks about terms," "the customer asks technical questions," "the customer says yes," and so on. These are all important buy signals. But the biggest buy signal is when the customer agrees to see you. The biggest buy signal is the sales call appointment.

Today's decision makers are usually too busy to see a salesperson unless the customer has a problem. Busy customers will not see a salesperson to chat, or talk about baseball. Busy customers are not doing a survey on the latest fashions salespeople are wearing. If the customer agrees to see you, it is because the customer wants something, needs something, has a problem. It is your job—the Rainmaker's job—to find out what that is.

You find out what the customer wants on a sales call. When the customer agrees to see you, he or she knows it is a sales call, knows that you are a salesperson. The customer knows something about your product. The customer knows something about your competition. Consequently, the agreement to see you is a setting of the table to do business.

Rainmakers understand this reality, and it gives them bedrock confidence to make the sale.

And always show up. Never blow off a sales call. Never be late.

• XIX •

Killer Sales Question #3

The customer says to you, "We are also in-terviewing [or "working with," or "buying from"] ABC company. They are a good company, and their prices are better than yours."

The customer is actually saying, "Tell me why I should buy from you." The customer already knows ABC is a good company. The customer already knows ABC's prices are better than yours. The customer knew this before he agreed to see you! So, why did the customer agree to see you?

The customer agreed to see you because there is something about ABC that makes the customer uneasy. You must underscore that unease.

Because you have preplanned the call, you are forearmed with how you and your company differ from ABC.

You answer exactly as follows: "Yes, that is a good company. Would you like to know our points of difference?"

This is a killer sales question.

Your response does not knock the competitor. To do so would be to impugn the intelligence of the customer. In fact, you do not even repeat the competitor's name.

The customer will answer yes because this is precisely the question he wants answered. He wants to know the difference between you and ABC so he can decide to go with you.

Your answer, your point of difference, will be forever what the customer thinks about you vis-à-vis the competitor. You will own that position.

Your point of difference (P.O.D.) should be

an offset to the competitor. It need not be better or worse than what the competitor does—just different. Your P.O.D. should be information—or a new slant—that the customer doesn't know. With new and different information, the customer can change his mind without loss of face or criticism.

The headmaster of an all-boys private prep school in Connecticut knew he competed with co-ed prep schools and high schools for good students. In meetings with prospective students and their parents, the headmaster would ask, "Where else are you looking?" Predictably, the name of an excellent co-ed school would be mentioned. The headmaster would look thoughtful (but would not nod his head, which would suggest approval) and then ask, "Yes, I know that school. Would you be interested in our points of difference?"

The headmaster would then say, "As you know, this school is boys only. Our point of difference is that our boys are not distracted from their studies because there are no girls in the class-rooms or locker rooms. Wouldn't you agree that more concentration on studies will make it easier to get into, and to succeed, at a good college?"

In an age when single-sex schools are more and more a rarity, this all-boys prep school not only survives, it flourishes. (Incidentally, if the "all-boys, no-girls" point of difference weren't meaningful to the customer, the headmaster had several more.)

"Me too" marketers are lazy, or noncreative, or have an inferiority complex. Rainmakers always find a difference. Rainmakers always invite customers to evaluate a point of difference. And the point of difference is just that—a difference. It need not be "better." The customer needs to see a difference, new information, so he can change his mind or change the minds of his colleagues. Some people like blueberry pie and some like rhubarb. Each is different from the other, not necessarily better. So when the pie customer says to the blueberry pie salesperson, "I like rhubarb pie," the salesperson responds, "Fine, would you like to know our point of difference? Unlike any other kind of pie, this pie is made with fresh, wild blueberries. Would you like to try a piece?"

Rainmakers sell that which is different.

· XX ·

Always Return Every Call Every Day

Returning phone calls is a basic courtesy. But not many people do it. Rainmakers return all calls every day. They return everyone's calls—customers, prospects, suppliers, job-seekers, parents. Rainmakers are not too big, too important, too busy for anyone.

Fast return of phone calls is a point of difference.

When you return a person's phone call, that person feels respected, important, listened to.

When you don't return a call, the caller feels you don't care, gets agitated, is less positive toward you.

There is no excuse for not returning phone calls. There are now voice mail, e-mail, car phones, cell phones, airplane phones. It is nearly always acceptable to leave a voice-mail message if the person whose call you are returning is unavailable.

Rainmakers love leaving voice-mail messages on weekends and before and after business hours. This shows that the Rainmaker is thinking about the customer and working for him or her all the time. It also allows the Rainmaker extra time to better prepare for the upcoming two-way conversation.

Voice-mail machines record the time and date of a call. Calls made at 6:15 A.M. and 11:10 P.M. are notable. Your customer will take note and remember.

• XXI •

Learn the "Miles Per Gallon" of Selling

Selling is a timed journey. The seller's destination is usually a quota, a goal, a necessary amount of revenue. The timing of the journey is often a fiscal year, a deadline to bring in revenue (e.g., to meet next month's payroll), or the sales cycle of the product.

This timed journey is like an automobile trip. The length of the auto trip is the number of miles between the start and the arrival. The sales journey is the dollar revenue to generate from the beginning of the selling period to the end.

The gas tank is the seller's available number of sales calls. The miles per gallon is the seller's call-to-close ratio. If the car has 25 gallons of gas, and gets 20 miles per gallon, the car can travel 500 miles. If the seller has 300 available sales calls in a year (number of selling days times average number of calls per day), and has a call-to-close ratio of 20:1* (i.e., 20 calls for every sale), the salesperson can make 15 sales. If the seller, in this example, cannot increase the total available sales calls, or improve his call-to-close ratio, then the sales potential is fifteen closes. . .not sixteen.

The Rainmaker understands this mathematical reality. Consequently, this Rainmaker plans up to twenty calls on a target customer, and does not call on more than fifteen targets.

---

*To calculate a call-to-close ratio, review last year's calendar (or the last few years) and count the actual number of sales calls made. Divide that number by the actual number of new sales.

The Rainmaker fishes where the big fish are. This means the Rainmaker calls on customers with large enough sales potential that, if closed, the resultant revenues will hit goal.

Less than 5 percent of all salespeople (and of all selling organizations) understand this concept intellectually, know how to calculate the math, know how to prioritize the probabilities, or have the discipline of the Rainmaker. Ninety-five percent of all salespeople will dilute themselves, by calling on too many customers and not allocating enough sales calls to close each sale. They will, in effect, run out of gas and not hit their goal.

Your available number of sales calls is your gas tank, your selling capital. If a home builder needs a mortgage of £100,000 to complete the house, and his banker only lends £80,000, what should the builder do, leave off the roof? It is better to lend £101,000 than £99,000. It is the same with selling. If it takes ten sales calls to close, don't plan eight. If it takes ten calls to make the sale, then it is better to make no calls than to make nine.

In the art and painting business, it once took 14 sales calls to get a collector to invest in a museum piece. Therefore, the call-to-close ratio was 14:1. If the art salesperson made 130 calls on 10 collectors, a 13:1 ratio, he would make zero sales. But if the salesperson called 14 times on 9 accounts, a 14:1 ratio, he makes 9 sales.

You must determine how many sales calls—or gallons of gas—you have in your tank. You must maximize your miles per gallon, your call-to-close ratio.

Work the math and the numbers will work for you.

Rainmakers don't plan a thirty-mile trip with twenty miles' worth of gas.

· XXII ·

Beware the Myth of Time and Territory Management

*T*here are books on how salespeople can optimize their time and territory management.
There are sales courses given every day that show
a salesperson how to get from here to there in the
least amount of time. There are speakers roaming
the countryside lecturing on how a salesperson
can best cover all the accounts in the territory.

Improving time and territory (T&T) management is an example of doing the wrong thing
right. Time and territory management is an ar-

chaic concept relevant for both door-to-door and route salespeople. Its relevance today is as a productivity tool used superbly by companies such as UPS and FedEx.

Time and territory management misdirects salespeople. The notion makes salespeople—and sales managers—believe that it is somehow wrong not to call on every good potential account in a territory. T&T sends too many salespeople to too many accounts resulting in too few accounts receiving the optimal number of calls to result in new closes.

Adherence to exacting T&T methods is a socially acceptable excuse for not hitting quota. Interview a sales force and you will inevitably hear salespeople complain, "My territory is too big."

How can it be a problem that a territory is "too big"? A real problem is if a territory, as measured in potential, is too small!

No one gets fired who brings in the business . . .regardless of how many accounts they call on. But lots of people get fired if they don't ring the cash register, despite working hard and dutifully calling on every account.

Rainmakers concentrate their calls on the highest potential accounts. Making 100 percent of your calls on one make-the-quota account is perfect T&T management.

• XXIII •

Always Taste the Wine Before
a Wine Tasting

*T*his is a lesson on planning to prevent failure. A wine tasting is a marketing event that wineries use to sell wines. A wine tasting is when people influential to the sale of wine—retailers, wine writers, restaurateurs—sample the product. Often the featured wine is a new one, or representative of a vintage just coming to market, or the first release from a new winery. If the wine tastes good, the influential tasters will be influenced to buy the wine or promote the winery.

Imagine the scene: The winemaker opens a bottle and pours an ounce or two into the glasses of ten wine magazine writers. To everyone's dismay, the wine is bitter. As the winemaker scrambles to open another bottle, the writers scribble. The second bottle of wine is fine, as are the next one thousand, but the damage is done.

Never assume something you can check. Pay attention to the details. Roll up your sleeves and get your hands dirty. If the project is important, every single detail is important. Broadway plays are exhaustively rehearsed. Experienced pilots always complete a comprehensive preflight checklist. Always check the projector bulb before making a presentation. Always check the microphone before giving a speech. Before you show your e-commerce website to a potential investor, be sure it works. Always precall plan a sales call.

A successful criminal attorney is called the "Furniture Mover" by bailiffs and other court personnel. This attorney leaves nothing he can control to chance. Before each trial, he visits the courtroom and, depending on his strategy, moves his client's chair closer to or farther from the jury. He places tables in the sunlight or the shade. He speaks aloud, checking the acoustics. He is tasting the wine. Unlike the hapless winemaker, when the Furniture Mover opens his case, his jury savors the product.

Rainmakers always test in private what they are going to sell in public.

• XXIV •

Dare to Be Dumb

*T*he biggest criticism of salespeople by customers is that salespeople don't ask enough
questions. Preplanned, practiced questions are ar-
rows in the salesperson's quiver. Good questions
get the customer talking, elicit information, allow
the salesperson to listen, and demonstrate to the
customers the salesperson's genuine interest. If
you don't do a proper diagnosis, you won't have
the correct prescription. Asking too few questions
is asking to fail. Hearken to the hotshot criminal

detective who related her biggest fear while conducting an investigation: "I am always afraid I will not ask the one important question that unlocks the case."

There are a number of reasons why too many salespeople ask too few questions. Ineffective salespeople don't prepare enough questions in precall. They don't write the questions down. They mistakenly think questioning is intrusive, impertinent. Ineffective salespeople assume they already know the answers. Some actually do know the answers, but that's irrelevant. And some salespeople are afraid that asking questions will diminish them, make them appear less expert.

All of these reasons are misguided and unacceptable. Customers love questions. Customers love to talk. Customers feel more secure with the salesperson who asks questions and listens and takes notes.

To the concerned customer with a need there is no such thing as a dumb question. So dare to be dumb. Assume nothing. Even if you have the perfect feel for a problem, ask questions so that the customer will know you understand.

Year after year, the top salesman for an adhesive company is a guy they call Columbo (after the television character). This Rainmaker has two degrees in engineering, plus a postgrad in mechanical engineering. He knows how things are made. He can take apart anything and put it back together. He knows springs, fasteners, seals, valves, blueprints, machinery.

Despite his years of experience and ability to instantly sort out a problem, he asks what his colleagues think are dumb questions:

- "How do you make this part?"
- "Why do you make it this way?"
- "How do you assemble the part?"
- "Why do you put that bolt there?"
- "How much do the bolts cost you?"

- "If you could eliminate one bolt per assembly with a less expensive method, that would save you money, correct?"
- "If I can show you how to fasten the assembly as well as it's fastened now, but with less cost to you, would you be interested?"

And so on to a close.

This Rainmaker asks enough "dumb" questions to become the highest paid salesperson in the company.

• XXV •

Always Do an Investment Return Analysis

*T*he investment return analysis is a powerful selling tool designed to get new customers and new applications. The investment return analysis calculates the economic benefits your customer will get from using your solution.

If you had two equal risk investment options, one returning 5 percent and the other 10 percent, where would you invest your money?

The concept of return on investment is simple, and it is the basis for nearly every business purchase decision. The Rainmaker knows this and uses arithmetic to show the customer how a £2,000 investment in a lathe will save £1,200 a year in reduced scrap. The reduced scrap is the benefit. The £1,200 is the dollarization of that benefit. In this scenario the customer gets a 60 percent per annum return on investment.

The greater the customer's return on investment, the more compelling it is for the customer to purchase—that is, make the investment. A properly calculated investment return analysis shows the customer what it is costing per day to go without the solution. In the lathe example, the customer gets £1,200 in savings returned. It is costing the customer £100 a month not to buy the lathe.

Showing the customer what it costs per month, week, or day to go without the solution shortens the sales cycle.

The investment return analysis helps your customer sell your solution inside his organization. There are usually eight to twelve hidden decision makers who need to say yes. Whether you are selling a pharmaceutical centrifuge for £500,000 or a stainless-steel bolt for £.05, your customer will need to justify the decision to go with your products. Your customer contact will use the investment return analysis to convince his or her colleagues.

The Rainmaker uses the investment return analysis to show the true cost (versus price) of the product. The Rainmaker doesn't sell the product. The Rainmaker sells what the customer will get from the product. The Rainmaker doesn't sell drills, he sells holes. . .and holes that are £.02 less expensive to drill.

• XXVI •

Never Forget: Everybody Is
Somebody's Somebody

*I*t was a typical luncheon place. There was a
counter, booths, and tables. The menu, a col-
lage of pictures of sandwiches and sundaes, was
laminated. The prices were reasonable. The wait-
staff included a bunch of summer-job high school
kids. The restaurant was in an affluent area.

One customer was upset about something. He
was angry with one of the young waitresses. He
was loud, rude, and nasty. Perhaps she had made
an error on the bill, or there was not enough B

in his BLT? Whatever it was, his overreaction brought tears to the teenager's eyes. The guy finally threw some money down and stomped out.

Three other kids watched what happened. One of the two boys behind the counter said, "I know that guy. I've seen him in my father's office."

Remarkably, each of the four high school kids had a parent who was a doctor. They found out from the boy's father that the angry customer was a salesman for a pharmaceutical company. Then and there, each kid planned to tell their parents not to do business with that salesman.

Being nice to somebody's somebody may not get you a client. But being hurtful to somebody's somebody could hurt you.

Rainmakers make friends, not enemies.

• XXVII •

Always Be on "High Receive"

Your job is to listen to your customer. You must accurately hear what they are saying and not saying. You must be acutely aware of all verbal and nonverbal signals. You must find out what the customer wants, needs, and doesn't want. You must learn how and when you can help the customer.

To do this you must watch and listen to your customer as sensitively and intently as military spy equipment monitors enemy movements and communication. Like the most sensitive of receptors you must be on high receive. Let nothing get by you; even the casual, offhand remark may offer clues.

Ask interesting questions. Listen carefully. Don't daydream. Don't mentally wander when the customer is telling you something you've heard a hundred times before. Don't start talking until the customer has completely stopped talking. Don't think about what you are going to say next. Take notes.

Turn off all cell phones and pagers before you meet with a customer. A ringing cell phone, locked in a briefcase, is an annoyance, is discourteous, and breaks concentration.

A woman was interviewing companies to remodel her bathrooms. She had carefully written down her decorating goals. She wanted to be sure the contractor she chose heard her idea, could offer suggestions, had the time to do the job, and would be affordable. The contractors she called were recommended by reliable references.

Each contractor arrived on time, took notes, asked questions. During a discussion of tile colors and sizes, one of the contractors' belt pager beeped. As he immediately moved to an outer room, he asked, "Is there a telephone here?" Minutes later he was back to the bathroom.

Two days later the contractors faxed their plan, schedule, and bid. The pager-beeper contractor's bid was the lowest by £1,500. The woman chose the higher bidder. She explained her choice: "Both companies were good. But if a page to call the office is more important than my time, then why would I do business with them? I should be the highest priority when I hire someone."

The three most important words in the Rainmaker's mind are "listen, listen, listen," and to do so on "high receive."

Rainmakers focus on the customers. Rainmakers give individual attention. To the Rainmaker the customer is king, and the sales call is an invitation to the king's court.

• XXVIII •

"Onionize"

To be successful, the Rainmaker must first get to the essence, the core, of what the customer needs. The Rainmaker must find the problem. The Rainmaker must understand all of the customer's concerns, desires, fears, and limits. The Rainmaker cannot prescribe until he or she diagnoses. The Rainmaker cannot turn the customer's need into a want until he or she knows how to put value on the customer's desired state. Just as a sous chef peels an onion layer by layer, so, too, the Rainmaker helps the customer get to the "heart of the matter."

Rainmakers use the word *onionize* as a memory trigger to remind themselves to keep probing, to keep asking questions, especially "why," "why," "why," and "why."

This is how a Rainmaker onionizes the customer:

"Tell me how the current situation is worrisome to you."

"Why is that important to you?"

"How is that important to you?"

"What are the consequences if this continues unimproved?"

"Can we try to find a solution that costs less than the problem?"

"How often does the machine go down or stop working?"

"What is the failure mode?"

"Why do you think that?"

"So the present seal occasionally loses its tolerance and then leaks, correct?"

"If you could get a new seal design that would eliminate leaks, would that be an answer?"

"Here's your new seal. If, after testing, it works as promised, is there any other reason prohibiting you from recommending it for full production?"

And fifty other onionizing questions are interspersed.

Rainmakers are akin to investigative reporters, detectives, psychiatrists, doctors, and archaeologists. They ask, probe, dig, diagnose, and listen. Rainmakers onionize to understand.

• XXIX •

If You Don't Care About the Answer, Don't Ask the Question

T his is about sincerity.

If you don't really want to hear all about every shot the customer took on her recent golf vacation to St. Andrews, Scotland, then don't ask. If you don't really give a hoot about the brilliant babblings of his new baby, then don't ask. If the customer's bronzed rugby shoes are not relevant to the sale, don't ask about them. Don't waste precious selling time—yours and your customer's—on matters not pertinent to helping your customer improve his or her situation.

If you ask about the picture of the sailboat, you may get an answer. And that answer will include every tack, every wind shift, every storm from San Diego to Fiji. And the customer will deliberately or unconsciously scuttle the call. Unless you are selling sailcloth, ask about the sailboat on your way out.

Rainmakers don't squander sales calls with unnecessary chitchat or entertaining conversation. Rainmakers are nice, engaging, informed, interesting, and interested. . .and always sincere.

Asking a question to flatter the customer is a form of insincerity, and is usually transparent to the customer. Customers are more impressed by intelligent, legitimate get-to-the-problem questions than they are by a phony inquiry.

• XXX •

Never Be in a Meeting

W hen a customer calls, they don't want to hear that you are in a meeting. Customers don't care if you are meeting with the president of the United States, the pope, or anyone else. Customers absolutely lose it when told you are meeting with others in your company. Customers don't care with whom you are meeting—with one exception: It is OK if you are meeting with another customer. It's OK because being with customers, and taking care of customers, is what you and everyone else in your company is supposed to do.

If you are in a company meeting and a customer calls, always take the call. A customer call is an invitation to help the customer, to get or keep his or her business.

In addition to never being in a meeting, you are also never sick. You are traveling.

You are never on vacation. You are traveling, or out of the country, and will return calls as soon as possible. Meanwhile, so-and-so is available to work with the customer.

You have never "left for the day." You are out of the office or meeting with customers.

You are never "out to lunch." You are meeting with a client.

You are never "not in the office yet." You are at a breakfast meeting with a client.

If the Rainmaker is temporarily unavailable,

the customer knows where she is. The Rainmaker is not "in a meeting," she is in court, on a job site, traveling to a customer, on a photo shoot, giving a talk at a convention, doing research . . .

• XXXI •

Present for Show,
Close for Dough

In golf, they say "drive for show, putt for dough." The idea is that huge smashing three-hundred-yard drives are less important than making a six-foot putt. A drive can land left or right in the fairway, or fifty yards short, and have less impact on the golfer's score than a putt two inches to the left or one inch short. Putting is unforgiving. A one-inch putt is equal to a one-hundred-yard shot. The professional golfers who make the most money are the best putters.

In selling, it is "present for show, close for dough." Don't depend on a fancy audiovisual or PowerPoint presentation to get the sale. Don't assume that giving a customer a colorful brochure is selling. Most customers don't say, "That video was so good I have to buy immediately."

Presentations, demonstrations, and engaging trade-show booths are a waste of money if they are not accompanied by a practiced, proactive strategy to get the customer to buy.

To some salespeople, a well-produced presentation is a crutch; to a Rainmaker, it is a tool. Some salespeople present and hope the customer decides to say yes. The Rainmaker presents and helps the customer to decide.

Rainmakers are cool and calm, and they don't miss many three-foot putts.

• XXXII •

Advice to a Baby-sitter

*B*aby-sitting—for pay—is a noble job, a noble profession. Baby-sitters look after their clients' most precious possession. Baby-sitters are teenage kids, au pairs, nannies, and day care centers.

In general, baby-sitters are in business for themselves. They get the jobs, do the work, and get paid. If they do a good job, they are rehired. As in many professions, excellent baby-sitters get paid more than the run-of-the-mill baby-sitter.

A teenage girl was getting ready for her first baby-sitting job with a new family, a new client. The teenager was ambitious, conscientious, and wanted spending money. The girl's mother asked her daughter if she would like some marketing advice about baby-sitting.

This appealed to the business-minded baby-sitter.

The mother gave the girl two tips: "One, no matter how bad the kids are, no matter how much trouble they cause, when the parents come home and ask if there were any problems, you tell the parents 'no problems, everything was fine.' And, two, leave the house a little cleaner than you found it."

This is great advice for the Rainmaker. Once a customer hires you to do a job, they don't want to know your problems doing the job. They don't care. Do a wonderful job, do it on time, do it on budget, don't complain, and give the customer a little extra. This is the blueprint for customer satisfaction and for continued sales success.

The teenage girl is now a Baby-sitter Rainmaker. She sells a relaxed evening and a neat house. She is always in demand.

• XXXIII •

Killer Sales Question #4

*C*ustomers need to be convinced that your product or service will work as claimed. The greater the investment, the greater the need for the customer to be sure. The newer the technology, the greater the need to test. Anything new—product, supplier, salesperson—usually triggers the need for some kind of proof.

There are various ways customers get the proof they need: samples, small assignments, product evaluations, product trials, demonstrations, references, beta tests, test markets. Marketers of consumer package goods use samples, for example, to get customers to know the product. (Wrigley chewing gum was launched in its hometown of Chicago by sending a pack of gum to everyone in the phone book.) Companies selling to other companies often use product demonstrations to convince.

Product demonstrations are often tricky to arrange. The salesperson must have the proper equipment, power supply, backup parts, recording sheets. Most important, the decision makers have to be present to view the demonstration.

When a customer asks for a product demonstration, the Rainmaker responds as follows: "We would be happy to give you a demonstration. If the demo is successful, is there anything else prohibiting you from going ahead?"

This is a killer sales question.

By asking "Is there anything else prohibiting you. . .," the salesperson is either going to hear some unresolved customer issues, or get an agreement to an action that leads to a close.

Rainmakers never leave product samples if the samples must somehow be tested. The Rainmaker knows that 95 percent of all samples left to be tested are still in a drawer or were tested incorrectly. The Rainmaker is always present when the customer tests the product.

Rainmakers never do a test or demo without first getting an agreement from the customers to go ahead with the sale if the test is successful.

Rainmakers never let the customer do the demo in his or her absence. If the customer makes an error, the salesperson suffers.

Rainmakers get buying commitments before they give selling demonstrations.

• XXXIV •

Give and Get

*I*n selling, if you give something, you should plan to get something in return from the customer. The customer knows you are a salesperson. The customer knows you are in business. The customer knows that you make your living by providing your product to solve, if possible, the customer's problem. The customer is ethical (otherwise be careful). The customer wouldn't be seeing you if you weren't ethical. The honest customer knows that he or she can't get something for nothing (even if their negotiations might suggest otherwise).

- If you give a sample, get an agreement to test.
- If you give a product demonstration, first get an agreement to buy if the demo proves the product works as claimed.
- If you give a brochure, get an appointment.
- If you give a discount, get more volume.
- If you give a free drink, get a next dinner.
- If you give a favor, get a due bill.
- If you give a solution, get paid.

David Ogilvy was the greatest copy writer in the history of advertising. Ogilvy was also an awesome Rainmaker: He brought in wonderful clients to his advertising agency. He was a master at giving and getting. One of David Ogilvy's memorable advertising campaigns was a series of ads he wrote to promote his agency, Ogilvy & Mather, in New York City.

Unlike the typical, predictable, and egotistical advertising that most agencies produce to promote themselves, Ogilvy "gave" his genius away. Instead of telling potential clients how great O&M was, instead of writing about himself, Ogilvy gave away how to do what his agency did.

One ad, headlined "How to Write a Corporate Ad," gave an accurate, detailed road map on copy points, layout, typeface, mistakes to avoid. Another, headlined "How to Make a Television Commercial," revealed Ogilvy's approaches and secrets.

One can imagine the internal debate at O&M: "If we tell them how we do it, they won't need us!" But the sage and savvy Rainmaker knew coffee companies made coffee not ads, and that automakers made cars not commercials. He figured potential clients would not go to his competitors and say, "Make me ads the way Ogilvy does it."

He knew that there is a huge difference between being shown *how* something is done, and then doing it at all, let alone well. If simply showing how to do something well were the answer, then simply watching Picasso paint or Andre Agassi play tennis or Julia Child make a soufflé would make everyone experts on everything.

Ogilvy's ads "gave away" this special knowledge and expertise, and got clients.

The Rainmaker gives to get.

· XXXV ·

Sell on Friday Afternoons

Anytime is a good time to make a sales call on a decision maker. Excellent selling times are before eight o'clock any morning and after three on Friday afternoons. Early-morning sales calls are good for two reasons: (1) there are less, or limited, interruptions, and (2) the customer's agreement to the unusual hour is a big buy signal.

Friday afternoon is a wonderful time to see customers. There are several compelling reasons for this. The customer is often more relaxed, more forthcoming, less harried, and less defensive. The customer is already thinking about a weekend at the beach or planting a garden. Some customers feel that if they make a decision on Friday, they can "sleep on it" over the weekend. To some customers, deciding to go ahead with your project provides a sense of accomplishment, gets something off the "to do" list.

If the customer agrees to see you on a Friday afternoon, particularly if she is leaving on vacation, be assured she thinks you can solve her problem, or she has already decided to buy. This is a high-probability sales call. But don't be overconfident. Be exceptionally prepared in order to close the order.

And the competition is not seeing customers on Friday afternoons. The other salespeople have started their weekend early. The other salespeople have left the arena, giving the Rainmaker an edge.

"Break the Ice" at the End
of the Sales Call

*T*here are all kinds of selling advice advocating the use of "icebreakers." An icebreaker is supposed to be some clever observation or comment by the salesperson at the beginning of a sales call that "breaks the ice" between the customer and the salesperson. The salesperson is coached to look around the customer's office to spot a piece of modern art or photos of kids playing soccer or a softball trophy and then to make an ice-breaking, bonding-type remark, "So, did you shoot that deer up there, or kill it with your car?"

There is no ice between a Rainmaker and her customer. You have an appointment, a scheduled time. The customer knows the subject of the meeting. You are there to help the customer. Your help is far more important than his collection of rowing medals—and both of you know that! So get to the point of the meeting, as expected.

You will connect personally with your customer if you ask sincere, diagnostic-driven questions and if you listen carefully and thoughtfully to the answers. On a first sales call ask questions that encourage the customer to talk about her company, her goals, her expectations. Customers reward salespeople who listen.

Communication between Rainmaker and customer is of great importance. Problems are discussed. Financial investments are considered and made. All parties are concerned that the decisions are correct and that good outcomes ensue. Although positive, the experience has energy, highs, bits of doubt, and closure.

If you had two minutes to get the sale, you wouldn't "break the ice" and comment on the suit of armor in the corner. So don't make the comment if you have twenty minutes to make the sale. Once the customer has made a commitment, when he or she is walking you to the elevator, this is when conversation about children or baseball or the hassles of business travel can be healthy and relaxing.

Icebreakers are for the Arctic Ocean, not for Rainmakers.

• XXXVII •

Use the Point System
Every Day

*T*here are four steps that are part of every sale.
They are:

1. Getting a lead, a referral, an introduction
   to a decision maker.

2. Getting an appointment to meet the decision maker.

3. Meeting the decision maker face-to-face.

4. Getting a commitment to a close (a purchase) or to an action that directly leads to
   a close.

Assign one point to Step 1, two points to
Step 2, three points to Step 3, and four points to
Step 4.

Work every day to get a total of four points,
in any combination of steps: four referrals, one
referral and one face-to-face meeting, one commitment, and so on. You can shoot for more
points per day if doable.

At the top of your daily to do list put "Get 4
Points." The key is to use the point system daily.
Don't wait until Friday and try to get twenty points.

If you tally four points per day, you will never
run out of prospects, your pipeline will always be
full, you will never have a slow period, and you
will always be making rain.

Try this system diligently for fifteen business
days, and then decide for yourself if it should become an integral part of your selling arsenal.

• XXXVIII •

A Shot on Goal Is Never
a Bad Play

Rainmakers go for it. They never negatively prejudge a sales event. Rainmakers never say "We're too small for that company," or "We'll never get an appointment with that guy." Rainmakers answer the question "Why should that customer do business with us?" and then they go for it.

Wayne Gretsky, the National Hockey League's greatest all-time scorer, said, "One thousand percent of the shots I don't take don't go in."

The Rainmaker knows one reality: If he doesn't make the selling attempt, there will be no sale.

A specialty metals salesperson had just finished a few days of unusual sales training. The training featured, to this salesperson's mind, radical ideas. The salesperson was told that the lowest price was not the same thing as the lowest cost, and that the highest-priced product could, in fact, represent the lowest cost of ownership to a customer. The salesperson was told that if the customer simply agrees to an appointment, then the customer is predisposed to buying. The salesperson heard a number of other selling notions that he knew, based on thirty years of experience, might work elsewhere but were bogus for "his" industry.

To prove the irrelevance of the training, the salesperson called on a potential customer who had never purchased from his company and, he assumed, never would because of his company's reputation for high prices, albeit good quality. To the salesperson's surprise, the customer agreed to see him. After just one sales call the "never will buy" customer stunned the salesperson with a £25,000 order. The salesperson now has a new attitude.

The 1980 U.S. Olympic hockey team—amateurs and college kids—had no chance against the mighty Russian squad—all professionals and veterans. And a last-second, ninety-foot shot was never going through the legs of the world's best goalie. But it did. And the United States won.

Rainmakers take shots on a goal.

· XXXIX ·

Don't Make Cold Calls

A cold call is when a salesperson visits a customer without an appointment. A cold call is a remnant of the days of door-to-door salespeople, when seeing as many people as possible was one way to succeed. Today, cold-calling is generally used by telemarketing people to prospect for customers.

Cold calls don't work. No busy decision maker has the time to drop what she is doing to see someone she doesn't know.

Cold calls are an intrusion and, to some, a sign of poor manners. A cold call is a gamble: You don't know if the customer is qualified, has a problem, or even if he or she is there.

Cold calls indicate poor planning. They indicate that the salesperson is not doing a good job qualifying leads or getting appointments. The old selling adage is instructive: Plan your work, and work your plan.

Instead of cold calls use the point system.

But what happens if, due to a legitimate emergency, a scheduled appointment is canceled at the last minute? It is Friday afternoon; you try not to be discouraged. You roll your eyes heavenward and spot a light burning in an office in a factory across the way. Maybe they are a prospect, you muse. What the heck, you think as you walk into the lobby, a shot on goal is never a bad play.

· XL ·

Show the Chain,
Sell the First Link

No one buys a chain link by link. No one goes into a hardware store and says, "Give me seventeen links," or "Let me have a box of links." People either buy the whole chain or they don't. It is the same with a sale. If the customer is shown all the steps in a sale and agrees to the first step, the customer has bought the chain. . .unless you break it.

Showing the customer the step-by-step, agreement-by-agreement process, from first sales call to purchase order, is a compelling selling technique. Only Rainmakers use this technique. Most salespeople either don't know all the steps, or don't understand the linkage, or don't plan strategically, or are afraid of showing their hand.

A super salesperson for a specialty chemical manufacturer is a champ at showing the chain and selling the first link, thereby selling the chain and closing the order. At her first meeting with a prospective customer she proceeds as follows: "Mr. Customer, we have a great deal of success in this type of application, always giving you, the customer, a positive dollarized return on your investment.

"Assuming we can give you such a return, would you like to know the typical steps involved in solving this problem?

"OK, good. First, we do a plant tour, and look at exactly how you assemble the product. Second, we get production samples of your product. We break them down and reengineer them, looking for ways to reduce assembly costs. Next, we work with you to develop an investment return analysis. Together we calculate how much money the recommended solution will save your company—or conversely, how much money it will cost you to go without this solution. Of course, you have to agree to the total amount of money you will be saving your company, OK?

"Good. Next, we do a test of our product here in your factory. If the test is successful, we go to a limited production run. All right?

"Good. If the test is successful, and the limited production run meets your criteria, we decide on a delivery date for your first full run production quantity. That's about it. Any questions?

"OK, great. That outlines the approach. Let's take that plant tour, OK?"

When the customer agrees to "take that plant tour" the customer has agreed to buy the first link . . .and, in effect, buys the whole chain.

The Rainmaker shows the chain, makes it clear how the phases in the sale are linked—from first agreement to purchase order—and then sells the first link. The first link is attached to the last link. Sell the first link and you sell the chain.

• XLI •

Don't Talk with Food in Your Mouth

*A*nd don't plop your briefcase on the customer's desk or conference table. Don't be late for meetings. Don't visit a customer if you are coughing and gagging and sneezing. Be sure your hands and clothes and hair and samples and car are clean. Stand up when an older person or a woman enters the room. Open the door for others. Offer to carry heavy items. Help lift a bag into and out of the overhead baggage compartments in airplanes. Say please and thank you.

Rainmakers use good manners all the time with everyone.

If you don't now have excellent table manners, you'd better acquire them. If you hold your fork like a gardener's trowel, shovel food into your mouth, make noisy slurping, smacking sounds, or chew and talk simultaneously, you will not get or keep customers. Bad table manners are a sign of a narrow or undisciplined or over-indulged upbringing.

Bad table manners are off-putting; they signal insensitivity to others, an overly self-interested person, and an incomplete education.

Drop your membership in the clean-the-plate club.

It was a "get business" lunch but one of the salespeople forgot. At one point the clicking of his spoon in a desperately empty soup bowl prompted the customer to remark, "If you scrape the porcelain off that dish, they'll have to throw it away." Unnecessary indigestion!

To Rainmakers, manners matter.

• XLII •

Killer Sales Question #5

Right now, this second, take a quick break from reading. Try and close this book. Close this book, put it down, then reopen and start reading. (Note: You are on page 121.)

You either closed the book or you didn't. Ask someone to toss you a coin, or a pencil, or anything. They either toss it or they don't. You can't "try" to do something; you either do it or you don't.

To close the sale, to get the final customer

commitment, the Rainmaker might say: "You've looked at everything. Your concerns have been answered. Time is of the essence. You've heard our recommendation. Why don't you give it a try?"

"Why don't you give it a try?" is a killer sales question.

The "it" is your product.

"Why don't you give it a try?" is not the same as "Why don't you try it?" or "Try it for a few days." To try a product for a few days is a trial. Getting a trial is a good selling strategy, but it is an interim step, not the final step, to getting a sale.

To give something "a try" is, to most people, a revocable act, a decision that can be reversed. It feels temporary, impermanent. Subconsciously, people feel that to try something is to sample, to test, not a commitment to a decision. There is an assumed escape clause built into an agreement to give something a try.

But people don't try: They act, they *do* something.

A super saleswoman sold a £1-million computer conversion that took eighteen months to implement by asking the customer, "Well, why don't you give it a try?"

• XLIII •

Love Voice Mail

*H*ave you ever thought: If I could just get the guy alone, I could sell him. If so, voice mail is one answer. Voice mail is a good selling tool.

Voice mail can be a selling opportunity for the Rainmaker. Voice mail gives the salesperson an uninterrupted period of time to communicate a meaningful dollarized benefit to the decision maker.

The objective of your voice-mail message is to

get the customer to call you back, or for the customer to take your next call or to want to meet you. The key to voice-mail selling is to leave a compelling message, something that resonates positively with your customer.

To be able to leave a good message the salesperson must accurately answer the question "Why should this customer do business with me?" You must answer the questions "Why should the customer call me back?" and "Why should the customer listen to me the next time I call?"

The answers to these questions must represent a significant benefit to the customer.

Here are voice-mail-usage guidelines:

- To answer the question "Why should the customer listen?" requires homework and analysis. To give the customer even an estimated sense of the dollarized value you represent necessitates precall planning.
- Brainstorm messages.

- Prepare your voice-mail message in writing. The core of this message should be a summary of the ultimate value you will bring the customer, and something you will use on a phone call, in a written letter, and in a face-to-face meeting. Preplan the message carefully. Keep it short; *no more than thirty seconds.*

- Consider using a third-party reference to set up your call and give you borrowed credibility. For example, "Dr. Jones in radiology at Saint Francis Hospital recommended that I introduce myself to you."

- Practice your voice-mail message.

- Be ready to convey your message if the customer picks up the phone.

- Speak slowly, clearly, and distinctly.

- Introduce yourself first. Be sure your name is easily understood. If you have a reference, state that person's name clearly.

- State how long your voice message will be.

- State the purpose of your call—to alert the customer to a dollarized opportunity now available.

- State the benefit and dollarized value.

- Suggest a limited time frame for your ulti-mate meeting.

- Give your telephone number, and speak slowly. Do not rush your telephone number. Always say "area code" before reciting your three-digit area code. When giving the seven-digit number pause between numbers. Then repeat the phone number.

- Thank the customer and tell her that if she doesn't get a chance to return your call, you will follow up.

To illustrate:

Good afternoon, Mr. Smith. A mutual friend, Jim Murphy, suggested I contact you. This message will take less than thirty seconds of your time. My name is Jeffrey Fox. The purpose of this call is to let you know of an opportunity that seems just perfect for you and your company. Based on analysis, you can reduce the manufacturing cost of the golf carts you sell by 12 percent, or approximately £900,000 a year. To see how you would save £900,000 a year will take about fifteen minutes. My number is area code 2-1-1, 9-8-7, 7-zero-zero-zero. Let me repeat that number: area code 2-1-1-, 9-8-7, 7-zero-zero-zero. If you can't reach me, I will follow up. Thank you very much.

When next you speak with your target customer, be prepared to say "Do you have your appointment calendar handy?"

• XLIV •

Park in the Back

Customers begin assessing salespeople in sec-onds. It is natural for some customers to build mental moats to protect themselves from making a decision to invest money in your prod-uct. They begin building mental defense systems and making the assessment as soon as they see you. So you want the customer to see you when you are organized and ready.

You don't want the customer to see you crab-bing out of a car, struggling into a jacket, straightening your skirt, taming your hair, fumbling with your briefcase. You don't want the customer to see you as anything but prompt and professional. You don't want the customer seeing you as vulnerable.

Never show vulnerability. Always be confident. Plan for the unexpected. Expect a curve ball. Stay calm. Remember the old poker-playing axiom: Never let them see you sweat. Never reveal a weakness, such as not feeling well. Customers don't care about your illness. If a customer asks how you are feeling, simply answer "Splendidly, thank you."

Park in the back. Get ready.

Rainmakers show up fit and ready.

• XLV •

Be the Best-Dressed Person
You Will Meet Today

"Friday is dress-down day," but not for the Rainmaker. The Rainmaker does not dress down, nor does he necessarily dress up. He dresses better than any customer he will meet that day. If the customer wears polo shirts and sneakers, the Rainmaker wears a blazer and loafers. If the customer wears slacks and a blouse, the Rainmaker wears a pants suit. If the customer wears polyester, the Rainmaker wears wool. Warning: You are not trying to one-up your client; you are letting the customer know he or she is important to you.

Don't succumb to the lure of "business casual." When you are trying to attract new business, nothing is casual. Your customer wants you to be "buttoned up" and professional.

But don't overdress. Don't overwhelm the customer with flamboyant sartorial splendor. Your dress should signal confidence, success, expertise, sensitivity, professionalism, and attention to detail.

Dressing with care flatters your customer. It is said that President Ronald Reagan had such respect for the Oval Office that he never entered unless dressed in suit and tie. The American people respected Mr. Reagan's respect, and perhaps it was one reason they reelected him in a landslide. Your respect for your customer will show, and your customer will appreciate it; your customer will reelect you, sale after sale.

• XLVI •

Why Breakfast Meetings
Bring Rain

Breakfast is an excellent time to do business with a prospective customer. A hugely successful Rainmaker, the late multibusiness owner Clayton Gengras of Connecticut, once remarked, "All the money I've made that stuck to my fingers, I made before eight o'clock in the morning." Breakfast jump-starts the day. Here's why:

- The customer knows the purpose of a breakfast meeting is not to discuss the World Series or to rate one cereal over another. When you arranged the meeting you gave the customer an idea of the purpose (which is some commitment by the customer to an action that leads to a sale). Consequently, when a customer agrees to meet you for breakfast, he or she is making an uncommon investment of time. That investment is a positive buy signal.

- Breakfast is usually less expensive than a business lunch or dinner. The menu is simple, requiring less time to make a selection, which means more time for discussion. You don't have to be concerned about alcoholic beverages.

- Breakfast saves your customer time. Choose a venue that is on the customer's route to work; this eliminates one of the "from office, back to office" trips associated with other outside meetings.

- Breakfast meetings are less vulnerable to cancellations. They happen before the customer's daily problems begin. And the customer is fresh, alert, and eager.

The choice of restaurant is less important for breakfast. It is hard to serve lousy tea and toast. Convenience to the customer is the important selection criteria. Don't go to a popular take-out place with a zillion people going in and out. Don't go to the local diner if it's a hangout for a motorcycle club. Don't go to the so-called power breakfast joints. They can be distracting. Those places are to show off; they are for show biz, not to do biz.

After you have received your customer's commitment and the meeting has concluded, don't walk out of the restaurant with your customer. Let your customer leave in peace and privacy. Excuse yourself to make a phone call.

One Rainmaker regularly schedules two breakfasts in a single morning. He jump-starts the day with two sales calls before most people even get to work.

• XLVII •

"Here's My Card . . ."

*D*on't forget to use your business card. To too many people the business card is so common, so trivial, that they forget its purpose. Business cards are to get and keep customers, to get into a customer's Rolodex, not to go into a bowl to win a free lunch.

Business cards should not be cute, cluttered, or clunky. Olde English script with curves and curliques is not classy; it is hard to read. Forget folding cards and fake Rolodex cards. Don't put every product you make and every logo in your organization on your card. Less is more.

A noted criminal attorney, a fantastic Rain-maker, consistently gave his card to bartenders, cabdrivers, waiters, construction workers—anyone. "Here's my card; if you ever need help, or anyone you know needs help, give me a call. We'll help you."

One real estate agent, for fifteen years the number one agent in her market, is always courteous but never bashful. "Here's my card. If you ever consider buying or selling real estate, give me a call. You will get special treatment."

A partner in an international accounting firm became partner in part because target clients got his card. "Here's my card. If you or your company want to reduce taxes and optimize cash flow give me a call. You will get our best people."

The owner of an upscale antique gallery didn't wait for customers to come to him. He often met business owners, and when he did, he handed them his business card. They were engraved, rich in tone. "Here is my card. Your elegant board-room is a wonderful place for our elegant antiques. We would be flattered if you would ask us for a recommendation."

Rainmakers know why business cards are called business cards.

• XLVIII •

Killer Sales Question #6

A complete understanding of the customer's needs, wants, concerns, objections, options, budget, and timetable is crucial to the Rainmaker. The Rainmaker must learn all that is relevant from the customer. The learning list is exhaustive and includes knowing the concerns of the customer's colleagues, determining the competitors, and gaining an intimate understanding of the problem.

The Rainmaker prepares for the input sessions with carefully crafted needs analyses and situation-understanding questions. No question is too trivial, too obvious, too mundane to ask. The goal is to diagnose the problem and to discover how your product or service will be of benefit to the customer.

Regardless of the quality of the questions, and regardless of the willingness of the customer to provide information, the Rainmaker always assumes he missed something. The Rainmaker always concludes an interview with a customer by asking one killer sales question.

The killer sales question is: "What question should I be asking that I am not asking." Variants, or follow-up questions, are: "Is there anything I have missed?" "Have I covered everything?" "Have I asked about every detail that is important to you?"

If you have covered everything, you're OK. If not, the killer sales question will unearth something that's important to the customer. The Rainmaker dissects the answer with probing follow-up questions.

"What am I not asking?" is asked by the most

confident, most customer-concerned, most professional of professionals. And good customers want to be asked this fantastic leave-no-stone-unturned question.

Rainmakers ask the questions others wish they had asked.

• XLIX •

Ten Things to Do Today
to Get Business

1. Send a handwritten note.
2. Clip and send an article of interest.
3. Talk to a satisfied client and ask who else you might help.
4. Send a thank-you gift to someone who referred you.
5. Give your business card to someone with influence.

6. Send a letter to the editor of a magazine your customers read.
7. Add fifteen people to your mailing list.
8. Leave a compelling voice mail.
9. Make an appointment.
10. Call a client you haven't talked to in two years.

Rainmakers do something every day to help their company get new business.

• L •

How to Recognize
a Rainmaker

*W*hat is the single attribute that characterizes the Rainmaker—the best salesperson? What distinguishes the markedly great salesperson from the merely good? Now, stop reading, close your eyes, and consider for a moment what is the single outstanding characteristic of a great salesperson. . . .

There are many "good" salespeople; there are

far fewer "great" salespeople. The good salesperson has a variety of success-creating habits and
attributes. The good salesperson:

- is organized
- calls only on decision makers
- does detailed precall planning
- always has a written sales call objective
- asks preplanned questions
- listens
- is empathetic with customers
- encourages and appreciates objections
- always dollarizes the value of the product
- asks for customer commitments

and a hundred other things, from being properly
dressed, to composing excellent communications,
to faultless follow up.

Those talents are all important.

But the one thing that separates the number one salesperson from all the rest is that the number one salesperson *sells more*.

When the score is tallied, it doesn't matter how hard someone worked, or how many brilliant memos someone wrote, or how perfect the monthly reports. It doesn't matter how clever the conversation, how hip the clothes, how smooth the style. The only score that counts is how much money has been generated.

If you have a Rainmaker, or Rainmakers, in your organization, you are fortunate. It matters not if your Rainmaker is a prima donna, an independent loner, or difficult to "manage." It matters not if your Rainmaker doesn't play by your rules, is indifferent to your policies, or is always late with expense accounts.

What matters is the Rainmaker's ability to ring the cash register, to put money in the till, to bring in new clients. As long as the Rainmaker obeys the laws of God and man, and stays within budget, you must let him make rain.

Tolerate your Rainmaker. Teach your Rain-maker. Train your Rainmaker.

Rainmakers bring the customers who bring the money that makes the organization flourish.

A RAINMAKER EXTRA:
HOW TO DOLLARIZE

You are in the paint store evaluating two brands of house paint. Brand A is £10 a gallon, and Brand B is £18 a gallon. Brand A has the lowest price, but Brand B has more pigment, thereby requiring one less coat of paint than Brand A. Which paint has the lowest cost?

To compare the true costs of each product, you must determine the total costs associated with each product. The process of making this evaluation is dollarization. Dollarization is figuring out—in pounds and pence—what each product is really worth to the customer.

In the house paint example, the customer or the salesperson or both calculate that ten gallons of Brand A is needed—a £100 job. Brand B can do the job with five gallons, or for £90. The labor cost for Brand A is twice that for Brand B. Brand B is the lowest net cost solution.

Price is the universal measure customers use to compare two products. However, if the customer's true goal is to get the lowest total cost, then focusing only on price is myopic.

Almost all sellers claim benefits for their products such as "faster," "stronger," "longer lasting," "superior quality," "more durable," "more efficient." Occasionally, the customer intuitively dollarizes the value of these claims and correctly selects the product that yields the lowest total cost. But more often, the seller, despite having the best solution, is reduced to fighting a price battle, because the seller does not know what "faster" means, or does not know how to translate "faster" into pounds and pence.

Sellers frequently have a difficult time placing a precise value on the benefits they provide.

For example, you are a salesperson for a gasket company. Your target customer buys gaskets to seal an engine component, and pays £.92 for each gasket. Your gasket is priced at £1.00. Because of a different design, your gasket is "more reliable": It fails eight times less often per thousand gaskets than the competition. Each failure results in a warranty claim that costs £25.00 to fix. What is the true price of your gasket? Can you dollarize the true cost of your gasket?

Here is how the Rainmaker dollarizes the value of the gasket, and every other product, using six basic steps:

1. Determine the Competition

State the other options your customer will be considering. Options could include an existing methodology, a competitor, or an in-house customer approach.

Example: The competitor is a proven supplier that sells its gasket for £.92.

2. State Your Benefit

State why your customer should do business with you.

Example: Our gaskets are more reliable.

3. Quantify the Benefit

Restate the benefit in numerical terms.

Example: "More reliable" gaskets means our customer faces eight fewer warranty claims per thousand products sold.

4. *Dollarize the Benefit*

Calculate the monetary value of the benefit.
Example:

Warranty Claims Avoided	×	Cost per Claims	=	Warranty Cost Saved
8	×	£25	=	£200

5. *Express the Total Dollarized Benefit in "Per Unit" Terms*

Calculate the portion of the total economic benefit the customer realizes from each unit he purchases.
Example:

Total Savings	÷	Number of Units	=	Savings per Unit
£200	÷	1,000	=	£0.20

6. Demonstrate the True Net Cost of Your Product

Show how the total economic benefit derived from each product reveals the true net cost (or true price) of your product.

Example:

Your Price	−	Savings per Unit	=	Your True Price
£1.00	−	£0.20	=	£0.80

Because of the total savings your product provides, the true net price per unit of your product is only £.80. In effect, when the customer gives you £1.00 for each gasket, you give back to the customer £.20 in warranty cost savings. Eighty cents is the number the customer should use when comparing competitors' prices.

Dollarization is the Rainmaker's edge. It is more effective to do the math and say "This air conditioner saves £14 a month in reduced electricity bills" than to simply say "This air conditioner is energy-efficient."

Three of the most important words in the Rainmaker's dictionary are dollarize, dollarize, dollarize!

A CASE STUDY:
MR. K.

*A*rguably the best salesman in the U.S. wine industry recently concluded an outstanding career as the chairman of one of the country's finest premium wine companies. For over thirty years, he personally sold millions of dollars' worth of wine, and many of those sales were made well before wine was as fashionable as it is today. Let's call him Mr. K.

According to Mr. K., this was his best sale:

In the fifties, Mr. K. was trying to sell wines

from an upstate New York winery to one of the most famous and finest establishments in New York City. This legendary restaurant was (and still is) frequented by a cosmopolitan and discriminating clientele, and it served only the best European wines. The restaurant was exclusive and catered to the desires of its patrons.

Mr. K. could not even get an appointment to see the decision maker. For six months the owner refused to see him. Mr. K. learned that the owner regularly ate lunch at the bar at three o'clock. A few days later, Mr. K. simply entered the restaurant and approached the owner while he was at lunch. The following sales call took place.

MR. K.: Excuse me for interrupting, Mr. Owner. My name is Mr. K. and my purpose is to show you why you should consider putting ABC Wines on your wine list. May I continue?

OWNER: I am having my lunch.

MR. K.: Mr. Owner, you meet with your customers every day when *they* are having lunch. I assure you, I do not wish to be a bother, but like you, meeting customers is also my job. This will take two minutes. May I. . .?

OWNER: Two minutes.

MR. K.: Will you please put ABC Wines on your wine list?

OWNER: No.

MR. K.: Why can't you?

OWNER: The wines taste terrible, and I don't like them.

MR. K.: Mr. Owner, I agree with you. The wines do not appeal to everyone. But if I can show you why that doesn't matter, would you consider them?

OWNER: I'm listening.

MR. K.: Thank you. The reason you should give these wines a try is not because you or I don't care for the taste, but because thirty-five to forty of your regular customers *do* like the taste. Mr. Jones and Mr. Smith like ABC Wines. And several times your waiters have been asked if you have those wines. This is a business opportunity worth £200 a week.

Mr. Owner, you should put ABC Wines in here because your customers will order and drink them. Isn't that reasonable?

OWNER: I will look into it and decide tomorrow.

MR. K.: That's fair enough. Thank you.

The next day, Mr. K. received an order for ten cases of ABC Wines. This was more than a token order, and ABC Wines have been on the wine list ever since. Every major restaurant in New York City soon put Mr. K.'s wines on their wine lists.

Case Analysis: Lessons in "Mr. K."

1. Mr. K. did his precall homework and determined when and where to find the customer.

2. Mr. K. stated clearly and immediately the objective of the sales call, and did so in question form.

3. Mr. K. was polite, always asking permission to continue. Said "thank you," "please," "may I."

4. Mr. K. concluded every statement in question form, asking for the owner's agreement.

5. When the owner raised an objection ("I am having my lunch"), Mr. K. reversed the situation. He changed places with the owner by saying, "You meet your customers every day when they are having lunch." Mr. K.'s message was "If it's OK for you to interrupt your customer's lunch, it is OK for me to do the same."

6. Mr. K. clearly stated the time investment to the owner (two minutes) and got an agreement to that time—the all-important first agreement in the sales cycle.

7. In his precall planning, Mr. K. learned about the owner's customers—the restaurant's patrons. Mr. K. brought patron research to the owner. Giving a customer new information allows the customer to change his or her mind without losing face.

8. Mr. K. used credible third-party testimonials: the comments from the waiters. This is powerful testimony because it can be easily verified.

9. Mr. K. asked for the order: "Will you please put ABC Wines on your wine list?" Mr. K. did what some studies indicate that 90 percent of all salespeople don't do: Mr. K. asked for the order.

10. Mr. K. answered the owner's objection ("no") with the ingenious "why can't you?"

The use of the word *can't*, as opposed to *don't*, or *won't*, is a subtle challenge of the owner's authority and power. "Can't" implies someone else has the power. This is unacceptable to many customers. If Mr. K. had asked "Why won't you?" the owner could have comfortably answered with a number of legitimate reasons, such as "We only serve French wines." To the question "Why don't you?" the owner could have responded "The wine cellar is full." But to accede to the question "Why can't you?" is to say "I'm powerless."

Mr. K. thought about and planned the exact wording of this response for weeks.

11. When the owner objected to the wines' taste, Mr. K. agreed that it was OK not to like the wines. Mr. K. did not debate. He deflated the rhetoric by agreeing.

12. Mr. K. used an "if I. . .will you" close (". . .if I can show you. . .would you

consider?"). This is good technique because the customer feels the burden is on the salesperson, not on the customer. But if the customer agrees to this proposal, and the salesperson delivers his promise, the customer is committed.

13. Mr. K. used a compelling reason for the owner to buy: Thirty-five to forty of the owner's patrons would order the wine. The owner both satisfies his customers and gets the dollarized benefit of £200 a week in extra sales.

   Mr. K. said, "Give these wines a try." Mr. K. was posing the purchase as a temporary, changeable, low-risk decision.

14. Mr. K. asked, "Would you consider them?" This is a variation of the killer sales question "Why don't you give it a try?"

15. Mr. K. eliminated the all-too-common customer/salesperson give and take. Mr. K.

took the focus off what the owner thought and put it on the restaurant patrons and waiters. This is called triangulation. The customer, the salesperson, and the third entity are the points of the triangle. Mr. K. and the owner can refer to the third entity and avoid parrying with each other.

16. Mr. K. used friendly words such as "consider" (twice!), "reasonable," and "fair." These words are noninflammatory and encourage mature discourse. The word *fair* is a strong selling word because it appeals to the customer's sense of fairness. Being fair leads to more objective, less emotional decision making.

17. Mr. K. received and acknowledged three commitments. The first commitment was the owner's agreement to two minutes. Mr. K. capitalized on that agreement by immediately asking for the order. Mr. K.

acknowledged the second commitment ("I'm listening") by saying "thank you." Mr. K. acknowledged the third commitment ("I will look into it") also by saying "thank you." Acknowledging and cementing commitments is strong technique.

The customer realizes he has agreed to something, and if the customer continues, it is a buy signal.

18. The goal of every sales call is to get a close or a commitment to an action that leads to a close. The customer's agreement to "look into it" was a commitment to an action that leads to a close. Ergo, a successful sales close.

19. What was Mr. K. actually selling? If he were selling wines, perhaps he might have brought a sample to taste (which would have killed the sale). But Mr. K. wasn't selling wine. He was selling the dollarized value (£200 a week) the owner would get

from featuring the wine. Mr. K. sold money.

20. Did Mr. K. break the rule of never making a cold call? Decide for yourself: The owner knew of Mr. K.——after all, he had spurned Mr. K. for six months. Mr. K. knew that a shot on goal is never a bad play. Mr. K. had nothing to lose.

Like every great Rainmaker, Mr. K. was brave and bold, courageous and calm. And like every great Rainmaker. . .you've got to know the rules in order to break them.

EPILOGUE

*T*hank you for reading this book. Now open the book to one or two random pages. Put your finger on a section and do what is written.

You will be farther on your way to becoming a Rainmaker.

ABOUT THE AUTHOR

JEFFREY J. FOX is the founder of Fox & Co., Inc., a premier marketing consulting company in Avon, Connecticut, serving over sixty companies in sixty industries. Prior to starting Fox & Co., he was vice president of marketing and corporate vice president of Loctite Corporation. Fox is the subject of a Harvard Business School case study that is rated one of the top hundred case studies, and is thought to be the most widely taught marketing case in the world. Fox earned his MBA at Harvard Business School. He lives in Connecticut.